Newport Ope ... *Society*

The First One Hundred Years

David Kenny

Published by Saron Publishing in 2021

ISBN-13: 978-1-913297-14-5

Saron Publishers
Pwllmeyrick House
Mamhilad
Mon
NP4 8RG

www.saronpublishers.co.uk
info@saronpublishers.co.uk
Follow us on Facebook and Twitter

Dedication

To my aunt, Eileen Kenny,

a member of Newport Operatic Society in the 1930s

Newport Operatic Society

The First Hundred Years

The Prologue

A few years ago, I was in the city of Dresden on New Year's Eve. I decided to go to a performance of *White Horse Inn* at the Staatsoperette. As a State Operetta, it has a key place in Dresden's cultural scene. Every seat in the theatre was full and the Staatsoperette has now moved to a new seven hundred seat complex nearer the city centre. Romantic light operettas, the music of Strauss, Lehar and Stolz and Benatzky are clearly alive and well in Germany. It offers the kind of 'middlebrow' escapism that was ever the backbone of Newport Operatic Society's productions over much of the 20th Century – a rich vein of theatre, now less popular here than it should be.

I first joined Newport Operatic for their 1970 production of *Calamity Jane*. *Pickwick* was my last show in 1998. In that time, we had gone from one two-week run in the month before Christmas and a spring concert, to two shows a year. At the start of my twenty-eight years with the Society, we specialised in big chorus shows. For many of these pre-war shows, such as *Desert Song* and *New Moon*, an audience no longer exists.

Sadly, in late November 1970, just before my debut on stage, one of the pillars of the Society, principal tenor Frank Davey, died. I never knew him but others, going right back to the early days of the Society, were still going strong and have contributed to this brief history. They recalled a time now lost to us. Theirs is a story of comradeship and occasional conflicts in pursuit of the highest artistic endeavour. It involved talented individuals and families over generations – the Duckhams, the Hollands and the Clissolds. Trevor Duckham, who was part of shows in the Tredegar Hall in Stow Hill and the Lyceum Theatre in the early 1900s, was joined by a sister, brothers, an uncle, a son and grandson.

Anyone who attempts a history of Newport Operatic Society faces a formidable cast list and memorable performances. To those whose highlights do not find a place here, my apologies. Nevertheless, I hope in these pages I capture something of the spirit of the Society and its times.

David Kenny
Tredunnock
March 2021

Savoyard Stirrings

References to Newport Operatic Society appear at the very end of the 19th century when the Musical Director, Frederick William (FW) Burpitt, employed in local government, and his leading man, John Green, a local schoolmaster, collaborated to promote Gilbert and Sullivan's Savoy operas. In 1900, there was a charity production of *HMS Pinafore* in an 'enormous marquee' at Llangybi Castle. FW Burpitt wielded the baton and John Green played Sir Joseph Porter. The Operatic Society numbered around eighty. It was a wholly amateur effort, noted a local critic – 'even to the painting of the scenery'.

By 1903, Burpitt and Green were ready for their most ambitious project yet. A newly constituted Newport Amateur Operatic Society agreed with Sidney Cooper, Manager of the Lyceum Theatre, on fronting a pre-Christmas Grand Charity Week.

The theatre, on the corner of Bridge Street and Cambrian Place, started life in 1867 as the Victoria Hall. After a disastrous fire in 1896, it re-opened as the Lyceum Theatre, much refurbished within its classical façade. It was modelled on West End theatres and richly decorated in gilt and cream. It could accommodate around 1,250 patrons and was Newport's grandest building. The programme was a showing of two Gilbert and Sullivan Savoy operettas – *HMS Pinafore* and *Trial by Jury* over three days, with three evenings of *Les Cloches de Cornville,* an early 19th century French comic opera, rarely revived today.

The Gilbert and Sullivan operettas were almost contemporary offerings, both having been written in the

Lyceum Theatre.

[Dando & Sons, Newport.

Taken from the Newport Year Book

1870s. For the *South Wales Argus* reviewer, the challenge for this amateur company 'gave proof of their courage'. The critique was generally positive but with a patronising touch.

There was 'a big gap between the best and the worst of the principals'. John Green in the lead role of the Judge had a 'true histrionic gift and bore himself like a serious actor'. The 'augmented orchestra, which included many amateurs, played their part well though occasionally a few of the players appeared to forget there was a conductor'. Green and Burpitt were jointly responsible for training the performers and conducting rehearsals. Green also doubled up as stage manager. The size of the chorus aroused comment: 'No professional company ever travelled with such a chorus – it could not be done! Although it was noticeable occasionally that members of the chorus did not move with the ease of professionals, their singing was magnificent – far better than the average professional "crowd".'

Attendances on Monday were poor but improved for *Les Cloches*. The cost and logistics for an amateur society of rehearsing and producing three operettas in a week must have been daunting and was not attempted again for nearly twenty years. In 1905, Burpitt left for a new life in Canada.

Still, there was some link with the 1903 productions and the unfolding story of Newport Operatic Society. Trevor Duckham, 'an imposing little figure' as midshipman Tom Tucker in *HMS Pinafore*, would play a part in the Society of the 1920s and 30s.

Left: Herbert Harte,
Chairman

Below: Harold Williams,
Musical Director

Below Left: TT Williams,
Secretary

Founding Fathers of
Newport Operatic Society

A Career of Promise

1921-1938

When peace returned after the Great War, the town of Newport still had no amateur Operatic Society. For two businessmen meeting in the autumn of 1920, this seemed a remarkable omission. Herbert Harte, Managing Director of the Mordey Carney Dry Docks and Ship Repairing Company, had called into Newman's Music Shop at the top corner of Skinner Street to purchase a record of *Yeoman of the Guard*. In the ensuing conversation with the shop's manager, Harold Williams, they not only discovered a mutual interest in Gilbert and Sullivan but also that both had been active in operatic societies in the North East of England. Was there the possibility of forming such a society in Newport?

A meeting was held over Newman's shop in November 1920, attended by a number of local people with an interest in the musical life of the town. The chair was taken by Arthur Sims, the conductor of Newport Choral Society and besides Harte and Williams, several stalwarts of the future society were present, including Charlie Giddings, R Graham White, who later became the Society's Chairman, Clarice Stokes, an accompanist for nearly twenty years, TT Williams and Norman Abraham. There followed an advertisement in the local press and a meeting held in the Town Hall Assembly Rooms at which it was enthusiastically agreed to form Newport Operatic Society.

Herbert Harte was elected Secretary and Harold Williams Honorary Musical Director. Harte approached the owner of the Lyceum, Sydney Cooper, to book the theatre for a week in December 1921. Although the Society was unknown and had no funds, Cooper was prepared to cooperate. True to the enthusiasm of its founders, the Society was to specialise in Gilbert and Sullivan Operas. The authentic guardian of the tradition was the opera company founded by Richard D'Oyly Carte who first brought Arthur Sullivan and WS Gilbert together and produced their work at the Savoy Theatre, London. It was fitting then that an old Savoyard, Lindsay Harman, was engaged as producer for the sum of £15. His pedigree was impeccable, having joined the D'Oyly Carte Opera chorus for their first production of *The Gondoliers* in New York in 1890, before becoming a Principal. In the 1900s, he started a new career as a producer for amateur operatic societies.

From the start, the Society was a happy combination of local people interested in music and prominent in business. Its reservoir of talent was mainly the flourishing local church choirs, with the non-conformist influence strong. Norman Abraham's father was Minister of Stow Hill Baptist Church. Accountant Arthur Holland, an influence from the earliest days, was a pillar of Victoria Avenue Methodist Church.

The first President was Sir Leonard Llewellyn, a local industrialist who lived at Llanfrechfa Grange, Cwmbran.

But the omens were not good. In spring 1921, the D'Oyly Carte Opera Company itself had a disastrous week at the Lyceum Theatre with their 'second' company. Could a home-grown amateur Gilbert and Sullivan Society do any better?

Monday night, 12th December 1921, saw the curtain go up on a performance of *The Mikado*. R Graham White was Pish Tush and Edith Gunter, a singing teacher always referred to as Madam, took the part of Yum Yum. RH Jones, taking the first steps towards a distinguished career in Savoy Operas, was Nanki Poo.

'Hopes were more than realised, prophesies more than fulfilled,' enthused the *South Wales Argus*. The chorus had a 'quality of freshness'. The critic thought Arthur Holland's Ko Ko was the 'great success of the production' and praised his singing, dancing and acting. Norman Abraham's Mikado was described as 'grimly sardonic' and 'consistent throughout' – attributes that were to be displayed to generations of Society members, both on and off stage. It was a triumph. Newport Operatic had begun 'a career of promise'.

Norman Abraham – the first Mikado

D.O'Brien.   N.Griffiths.   L.Barry   K.Deane.

M.Witts.   O.Newman.   H.Williams.   M.White.   M.Jones.

Ladies Chorus, The Mikado

The Society followed its initial success with a performance of *The Gondoliers* in 1922 and by 1923 was ready for *Yeoman of the Guard*, perhaps the most demanding of the Gilbert and Sullivan operas. The *Argus* considered it the best performance of its short career but cautioned that 'if performances are to be a financial success, the cheaper parts of the House will have to be occupied better'.

Arthur Holland – a future Musical Director, as Jack Point in the 1923 performance of Yeomen of the Guard

Lack of patrons in the balcony were still a problem in 1924 when the Society performed *Iolanthe* - a good chorus show with up to twenty-five men on stage. The critics appreciated it - Newport Operatic Society was quickly becoming an institution.

Arthur Holland, who had received great plaudits on stage in 1921, was appointed Musical Director in 1926.

WJT Collins on stage at the last night of a performance

The association with the *South Wales Argus* was strengthened with the appointment of WJT Collins, the rugby columnist 'Dromio', as President. Known as Colley, he was remembered for his monocle and for his kindness. When leading bass Gordon Leonard was taken ill during the performance of *Rose Marie*, he rang every day to find out how he was and posted a bulletin for members.

In 1935 the Society took the momentous decision to switch from Gilbert and Sullivan to what was considered at the time as the more modern type of musical. The 'old shows' were not proving a box office success - in particular, the Society's production of *Merrie England* in 1930 had drained finances. The Committee judged that there was a desire for spectacular shows as originally staged in London. Professional companies were reducing runs outside London and the Operatic Society saw an opportunity.

Desert Song of 1935 was considered as one of the Society's highlight performances. Newport was the first amateur company in Wales to attempt it. The impresario who owned the musical insisted that Harry Winton, the stage manager at the Theatre Royal, Drury Lane, produced it. He brought his experience of the first UK production of *Desert Song* at Drury Lane in 1927.

In 1936, there was more drama off stage than on. King Edward VIII was due to broadcast on 11th December regarding his future and the relationship with Mrs Wallis Simpson. It was during the run of *The Vagabond King*. Recognising this, the theatre agreed to interrupt the performance and relay his speech to the audience. A loudspeaker van toured the town to reassure those attending that they wouldn't miss out. The curtain came down and the King announced his abdication. The comedy scene that followed was punctuated by sobs from the audience. The libretto which included cries of 'down with the King!' did nothing to improve the atmosphere!

In 1937 and 1938, the Society moved to the Empire Theatre in Charles St, Newport. With room for 2,500 patrons, it was double the capacity of the Lyceum – indeed, there was said to be more money in the Circle of the Empire than the whole of the Lyceum.

As the 1938 programme for *New Moon* put it: 'Of the original company who stood trembling in the wings on the opening scene of *Mikado* in 1921, only one - Wilf Davies - remains on the active list.' This chorus stalwart had appeared in every one of the 108 performances since the beginning.

Many, however, continued to be involved in Committee and four members - Aileen Davies, R Hugh Jones, Richard H Dunn and Bernard Maher - had left to join the D'Oyly Carte Opera Company. They continued to send good luck telegrams to their old Society on the eve of productions.

The Newport Empire –fire engines tackle blaze on 7ᵗʰ January 1942. Hours before, world famous pianist Charlie Kunz gave what was the final performance at the theatre.

After the War

Promise Fulfilled

There was a general audition after the war. The emphasis was on youth and some old established members failed to get back. In many ways, it was a new society but the choice for 1948 was an old favourite – *Desert Song*. A young John Richards was given the part of The Red Shadow. As in 1935, it was a watershed show.

Principal cast of Desert Song

The Empire Theatre had burned down on the night of 7th January 1942 so it was back to the Lyceum. *Desert Song* was to break all box office records. The queue started to form at 4am on the Monday when seats were first offered to the public. By opening time, there were already one thousand people. First in the queue was Goff Page who made a lengthy block booking of four hundred seats. Many regular supporters were unlucky and complained bitterly to the *South Wales Argus*. In a twelve-hour booking period, practically all the seats were sold for a show which was still two weeks away.

Rehearsals continued but a few days before opening night, disaster struck. The producer Harry Winton was taken seriously ill and could not continue. A girl who was acting as a prompt and was due to produce the pantomime to follow the operatic show was asked to step in - the Maisie Griffiths era had begun.

Maisie Griffiths, despite being based in London, came from a distinguished North Wales family. Her father had been a Liberal Member of Parliament for Wrexham and really did know Lloyd George. Maisie even recalled the great man pushing her around in a pram.

She was young but already had wide theatre experience. She had been a classical dancer, appearing for a time with Pavlova's Corps de Ballet. Maisie recalled her audition aged 16 or 17 before Anna Pavlova , the greatest Russian ballerina of her generation, and Anton Dolin, a founder of the Royal Ballet. She couldn't do the instruction set by Dolin and challenged it, receiving support from an unlikely source. 'The girl's quite right,' said the great Pavlova. Maisie was always unorthodox – 'I liked acrobatic as well as classical dancing.' Later, Maisie turned to cabaret and speciality dancing and had begun to produce shows. During the war, she joined ENSA, entertaining troops in France, North Africa and the Far East.

She was an unlikely producer of operatic shows. She confessed, 'I can read music and la-la a tune but I've always had to kid people I could sing a little, while at the bottom of my heart, I knew I couldn't.'

She arrived from London and started the Sunday dress rehearsal not knowing a soul. 'The company looked at me as if I had arrived from another planet.' Goff Page saved the day by asking her to have a drink in the committee room and then she met everybody. The Society immediately took to her. Joan Weatherley, a new member, (later to become the Society's President), recalls she was 'a super dancer - we all loved Maisie'.

The show was a great success. John Richards was a convincing Red Shadow, and Goff Page as Benny was partnered for the first time by Phyllis Brewer in what was to become a highly successful comic duo. The committee was clearly impressed by Maisie who was a producer in her own right for the next show.

Maisie Griffiths brought to the Operatic Society the ability to 'see a picture'. She had a good sense of colour and the costumes always blended well. 'She always made sure the show was well lit,' remembers Goff Page.

The 1949 show was well worthy of her talents. *Nina Rosa* was expensive and not often produced. The ancient Inca city of Cuzco had to be created on the Lyceum stage. Massive feather headdresses were required for the ladies chorus. The show was completely new to Maisie and the role of Nina Rosa was entrusted to nineteen-year-old Rosemarie Jones, later to join the D'Oyly Carte Opera Company. The result was a triumph. The Society enjoyed one of its finest opening nights. 'The Cave of the Incas tableau would be a credit anywhere,' enthused the *Argus* critic.

In 1950, the Society again gave young talent a chance when they picked a twenty-three-year-old soprano - Betty Turner, later Betty Hodgkinson, for the lead in *Countess Maritza*.

Betty Turner did not have a really outstanding voice and could not read music but her singing, recalled Maisie, was 'very sweet and accurate'. She was also a good all-round performer possessing, as the Countess, 'an infectious charm

The Cave of the Incas

Put Me Among the Girls
Maisie with the ladies chorus of Maritza

and stage presence', according to one critic. These qualities were to make Betty Turner perhaps the best remembered female lead of Newport Operatic's post war period.

. Newport Operatic Society continued to prosper in the 1950s. In 1952, the traditional first week in December was extended to ten days and the following year, to two weeks. In 1956, Frank James returned to Newport, somewhat jaded with a career in professional radio, and took the lead of Rudi in Ivor Novello's *The Dancing Years*. Seeing Goff Page in operatic performances as a child had made a great impression - he joined Goff on the operatic stage and was later to follow him as the Mayor of Newport's Secretary. *The Dancing Years* was something of a tonic.-'One of the best two weeks of my life,' says Frank. 'People stopped you in the street - you really felt like a star.' He recalls Maisie as having 'no favourites' and being 'very scant with her praise'. This was very much part of her strategy. She knew that people talked to one another and relations suffered when you singled people out for special attention.

For *The Dancing Years*, a piano appeared in the pit for the first time and new junior accompanist Dorothy Atwell Clarke was proud to play along. Frank James, as Rudi, played the piano on-stage. The precedent having been set, the piano continued to be a fixture in the orchestra for future performances.

There was, though, no denying the special appeal of some. Frank Davey, not a great actor but endowed with a soaring tenor voice, the amiable buffooning of Ted Grainger, the comic touch of Goff Page. John Jenkins, the bass soloist, was a dress designer and invaluable in preparing a set – 'wonderful at draping,' remembers Maisie. His stagey manner used to change dramatically before a performance. Arriving at the theatre early, he used to withdraw to get into character. John's rendering of *Ol' Man River* in the 1953 production of *Show Boat* is still remembered. He was clearly a man of contrasts - as a bobby on the beat, he regularly patrolled some of the roughest areas of dockland Newport during the war.

The team: Arthur Holland, Maisie Griffiths and Norman Abraham

The Society had at its helm a formidable triumvirate -
Maisie Griffiths as Producer, Arthur Holland as Musical
Director and Norman Abraham as Secretary. The Producer
and Musical Director had a considerable professional
rapport but did not always agree. Maisie recalls that she
wanted to select a certain soprano for a part. It was clear
from her audition that she was the best but Arthur, always
the stern moralist, did not agree. She was, he said, 'an
unsuitable person, there was something in her past'. Maisie
insisted and won the day.

The 1960s

The new decade was to see changes. In 1960, the Society performed *Rose Marie* - its last show on the professional stage. Arthur Holland spoke movingly from the footlights: 'It is with a feeling of sadness and regret that I heard the last chorus and realised that never again shall I come out here to conduct.' It was left to Secretary Norman Abraham to strike a positive note: 'This is not a funeral, we shall make a fresh start elsewhere and we are optimistic about our prospects.' The old Lyceum Theatre was sold and partially demolished the following year.

In 1961, Newport Operatic Society found a temporary home at the Little Theatre, Dock Street - a former chapel and the home of Newport Playgoers. The stage was small and *South Pacific*, with its many scene changes, posed added difficulties for Maisie - in this converted church, there was no chance of 'flying the scenery' into a loft above the stage, enabling quick changes of sets. As usual, the problems were overcome. The *Argus* reported that the relative smallness of the stage 'did not appear to inhibit the cast at all'. *South Pacific*, which brought together the lead partnership of Margaret Shead and Ian Frost, was regarded as one of Newport Operatic's best ever shows.

With kitchen sink dramas at their height and the Beatles waiting in the wings of popular music, the Society was still attracting good audiences with romantic shows like its 1962 production of *The Dubarry* which brought the popular duo of John Tobin and Monica Richards together. John Tobin, a Newport teacher in his early thirties, was 'admirable in looks and voice', said the *South Wales Argus*.

Margaret Shead and Ian Frost together in the 1964 performance of
Annie Get Your Gun

But Newport Operatic Society was no longer the automatic choice. The Standard Telephones and Cables Operatic Society was founded in 1958 and quickly gained a reputation. They had their own stage and the backing of the company. Two years after John and Monica's successful debut with Newport Operatic Society, they were starring as Paris and Helen of Troy in Standard Telephones production of *La Belle Helene*. In September 1964, they took the show to the Waterford International Festival of Light Opera. The production came First to rave reviews from the adjudicator, with John winning the best male performer award. In January 1965, there was a recording by the BBC - unprecedented recognition for an amateur operatic society. John was soon in demand as a lead for new local societies

John Tobin and Margaret Shead-Gwatkin in the 1982 production of La Belle Helene

like The Graig, and Caldicot. Ten years later, he would be back with Newport Operatic Society, still taking lead roles in a new venue, the Dolman Theatre, created within the Kingsway Centre.

In 1963, the Society looked forward to its production of *The Belle of New York*. All the omens were good. Early sales were the biggest since the Society began staging shows at the Little Theatre and a first Saturday matinee was arranged.

But a few days before opening night, the Society was dealt a sad, staggering blow. Arthur Holland, whose performance had almost been taken for granted, died. It was Billy Martin, who had played in the orchestra in the 1921 performance of

Mikado, who mounted the rostrum as conductor. Shortly afterwards, Maisie announced that, for personal reasons, she was restricting her out of London commitments and could no longer undertake the Society's productions. Norman Abraham had already given up the job of General Honorary Secretary in 1962, after nearly forty years of service in this role, becoming the Society's first Honorary Life Member.

The formidable triumvirate was no more. It was indeed the end of an era.

A Social Highlight

Operatic shows were part of the social life of 1930s Newport. There was the Civic Night, a special Masonic Night, a Military Night attended by the Society's Chairman Lt Col Gwynne C Thomas and officers, not only from Newport Barracks but sometimes the Royal Horse Artillery based in Bath. They occupied the best rows in the Circle or Stalls and were often joined by Lord Raglan and Viscount Tredegar. Fridays were Theatre Night when the audience, which included the subscribers, were expected to dress up - evening dress with gloves for the ladies and tails for the men. For the performers, this was always a difficult night when the audience tended to 'sit on their hands'.

Newport Operatic Society continued to enjoy the patronage of prominent local people into the 1960s. Lord Leighton of St Mellons, Director of the family ship-owning company, WH Seager of Cardiff, and Vice Lieutenant of Monmouthshire, was one. In December 1962, his wife Marjorie wrote to Maisie:

I cannot resist the urge to send you a note to say how greatly Lord Leighton and I enjoyed the performance of The Dubarry last evening... The Society has once again excelled itself. (see overleaf)

The Society might have drawn its membership from the 'leafier' parts of the Borough but it grasped talent and enthusiasm from wherever it could be found. A young Charles Giddings, an ardent Gilbert and Sullivan fan, was there in Newman's shop when the Society was first founded. 'I am a Pill Boy,' he proudly used to say and took part in seventeen productions. He was, above all, a team player and

29

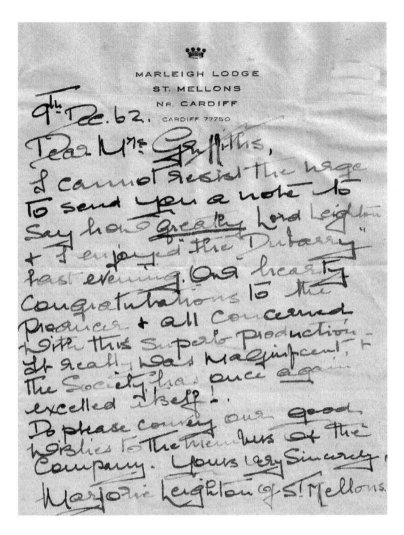

had little use for anyone who was not prepared to give of their best for the show. He was the Society's Chairman from 1958 until his death in 1963.

The Society at Work

In the pre- and post-war years, Newport Operatic Society came first. It was the only such local society. New members joined simply because it was Newport Operatic Society. Before the war, the annual cycle began with an advertisement for singers in February. Auditions were over three or four nights. The committee would see perhaps forty candidates and accept four. Joan Weatherly remembers walking the full length of a room towards a semi-circle of committee members. Arthur Holland got the range of voice. If you were accepted, you were a singer. All the chorus were potential soloists. Even so, soloists of the calibre of Frank Davey were happy to sing in the chorus. If you had the lead one year, you would not expect to get it the next. High standards were expected of members and the Society could afford to be choosy. It was always Norman Abraham's view that ladies of the chorus should give up when they reached the age of forty. There is no evidence that this advice was heeded then, any more than now!

In February, the committee would go up to London and see a few shows at the Scala Theatre and estimate some costs.

The Society used a number of venues for rehearsals - the YMCA, the Bridge Inn, St Woolos School and even the Synagogue - but the strict discipline was always the same. Norman used to say that when it came to the Society, you were 'either in it or out of it'. Rehearsals started at 7pm and Norman would stand on the steps of St Woolos School. Two minutes past was considered late and could earn a rebuke.

Rehearsals did, however, have their social side. There was usually a break with tea provided by the ladies. One of the men usually took a new member under his wing and made some introductions. Some felt the Society in those days was welcoming and without cliques. Other new members like Dorothy Atwell Clarke, who joined as an accompanist, had a less easy initiation. 'For the first few rehearsals, no one even spoke to me - the accompanists were certainly never offered tea.'

Before the war, most of the Society could read music and by the summer break, the show was basically learnt. Arthur Holland always knew everybody's lines and music from very early on. He was, according to Frank James, a lead in the 1950s, 'the most professional amateur'. The secret of success was hard work, with Norman and Arthur, 'bark and bite', striving for perfection. The last week before the show, the cast could expect to be called every night.

Every effort was made to make sure a show was well presented. Producer Maisie Griffiths would sometimes freshen up the furniture on stage. The ubiquitous Charlie Giddings was a professional signwriter and could get the paint cheap! Maisie spent days making flower baskets for the 1957 performance of *White Horse Inn* with the ladies of the chorus - paper carnations with hairnets to keep the flowers in.

On the nights of the show, the chorus were expected to show the class and style which audiences associated with Newport Operatic Society. Joan Weatherly epitomised this tradition and recalls the meticulous attention paid to costumes. Costumes were normally collected on Friday. On Saturday morning, she would meet the rest of the ladies chorus in shops in the centre of Newport - Woolworths, London House or EG Taylors – 'trimming up' their outfits. Saturday afternoon was for sewing. Whites were always washed and starched. On Sunday, everything was pressed and put on hangers. The men too aimed to look their best. Goff Page provided his own tails and was always immaculate.

Working in the Lyceum was an experience. To old members, it had the glamour of a 'proper theatre', seating over twelve hundred people. You could smell the greasepaint. Conditions backstage were Spartan and accommodation distinctly hierarchical. Level with the stage was the principal ladies dressing room, above them the dancers, and above again, the ladies chorus –one room each for sopranos, mezzo sopranos and contraltos.

The top changing accommodation was reserved for the gentlemen - principals and chorus. They were a long way from the stage and the stairs were narrow and difficult. There was no tannoy system and the cast relied on call boys to summon them in time.

None of the cast did their own make-up, though the dancers looked out for themselves. In the 1950s, a London-based perruquier, Frederick Sabine, provided wigs for the Society.

Discipline was still maintained in the theatre. Joan Weatherly's mother used to meet her at the stage door with clean gloves and spats - no one not connected with the show was allowed in the theatre. Norman was as ubiquitous as ever. One day, he caught Joan cutting across the stage to the dressing rooms. 'Don't you ever do that again,' he boomed. 'No one walks across an empty stage.' She didn't argue – well, no one ever did!

Romance – On and Off Stage

Operatic society people are natural romantics. Couples drawn together on stage often discover a natural chemistry – a squeeze of the hand or a furtive kiss in the dark wings are not unknown. Sometimes romantic overtures are unappreciated. Ladies of the chorus are sometimes forced to deliver a sharp rebuke, and sometimes an elbow, to the more annoying 'pests'.

John and Jean on stage

Rarely do romances survive beyond the final curtain but few were surprised when long-standing leads of the 1970s, John Walters and Jean Butcher, tied the knot.

The AGM was sometimes dangerous for singles, particularly in leap year. Chorus stalwart Chris Davies received an unexpected proposal of marriage at one 29th February AGM in the 1990s. 'He said *Yes*,' screamed the ladies –well, perhaps this eligible bachelor was a little too wily!

Sometimes love blossomed more gradually. Lorraine Pitt had become hooked on the Operatic Society since her mother Joyce took her to see *South Pacific* in 1961. Joyce joined in 1965, followed by Lorraine. Both worked, front of house and backstage, with the Society's Secretary Eric Lane. Lorraine became particularly close to Eric and his wife Enid who took cameo roles in productions. It was Enid's dying wish that Lorraine look after Eric when she was no longer around. It was a leap year when Lorraine proposed to Eric who was twenty-five years her senior and initially, he put all kinds of obstacles in the way. Eventually love won out. Eric observed the old-fashioned courtesies and sought mum's permission and in October 1984, Lorraine and Eric were married. Lorraine didn't wear a wedding ring to rehearsals and it was only at the AGM in February 1985 that Eric formally announced it - the 'proper time' to tell everyone!

'After ten years of togetherness,' says Lorraine, 'we had truly fallen in love.'

Eric and Lorraine Lane

Changing Times

For the old guard, the 1960s and 70s were unsettling. In 1967, Newport Operatic moved productions to the new Dolman Theatre, designed and equipped to full professional standards and with a capacity for just over four hundred patrons. *Kismet* was the first production.

Good productions followed. In 1973, seventeen years after Dorothy Atwell Clarke became an almost invisible recruit as a junior accompanist, she took up the baton and her trade mark white gloves as the first female Musical Director of Newport Operatic Society. The show was the same, Ivor Novello's *The Dancing Years,* but Jon Styler, as leading man Rudi Kleber, was a fine pianist and had no need of the piano in the pit!

Yet for others like Bill Clissold, the Society's President in the 1980s, shows like *Kismet* and *Pajama Game* were too modern. Gordon Leonard, involved from the early Gilbert and Sullivan days, felt that performances in the latest *Yeoman of the Guard* were not sincere or serious enough – 'There is only one way to play G and S characters.' Maisie Griffiths returned in the 1970s to produce a few more shows, including the 1975 production of *Desert Song*. It was the last of the two-week runs at the Dolman and sales were encouraging enough for a Saturday matinee. Ian Frost gave a relaxed and confident performance - the finest Red Shadow of his generation.

Despite its success, it was the swansong for the great romantic shows. That great Jerome Kern classic *Showboat,* which Newport Operatic Society reprised in 1988, fell out of favour soon afterwards. Half the chorus 'blacked up', an expedient considered demeaning and unacceptable by the turn of the 21st century. Local authorities were increasingly intervening to censure productions which did not have an authentic black chorus – a luxury to which few amateur societies could aspire. Despite a wonderful score and a progressive Oscar Hammerstein narrative with a plea for racial harmony, *Showboat* has virtually disappeared from the amateur stage.

Tastes were transforming and so was the Society. Maisie bemoaned the 'lack of stagecraft, lack of fun, with fewer gentlemen on stage'. The times indeed were a-changing. The Society's current Chairman, Chris Edmunds, sums up the problems - dwindling audience figures, escalating production costs and a dwindling cast and chorus.

Men's chorus of South Pacific 1973

Newport Operatic Society is intertwined with the history of our town - as 'Old Newport' as the Town Hall Clock and the Transporter Bridge. Despite all the problems, the Society still exists, hopefully to enliven the dark days before Christmas with light and magic for many years to come. Maybe they will create their own legends. It is, though, hard to see a group of amateur performers ever again being as prominent in the cultural life of a town as Newport Operatic Society was for much of the 20th Century.

Dorothy Atwell Clarke – long-standing Musical Director from the early 1970s and who 'guested' for many other local operatic societies. She took Cwmbran Operatic Society's 1997 performance of Chess to the International Festival of Musical Theatre at Buxton where Dorothy was named Best Musical Director. There followed an invitation to the Royal Albert Hall, conducting a large orchestra and cast in excerpts from Chess in Concert. Dorothy remains President of Newport Operatic Society

With particular thanks to:

Norman Abraham, Bill Clissold, Goff Page and Sue Burgess (Clissold)
Maisie Griffiths, Dorothy Atwell Clarke and Lorraine Lane (Pitt)
Frank James, Gordon Leonard and Christopher Edmunds
Joan Weatherley, Bunty Duckham Jones, Margaret Shead Gwatkin, Ray Lewis and Val Salter
Nigel Young
Newport Central Library
National Operatic and Dramatic Association (NODA)
South Wales Argus

Newport Operatic Society – Milestones on the Journey

- ❖ **1900** A group with the title of Newport Operatic Society produce *HMS Pinafore* in a marquee at Llangybi Castle
- ❖ **1903** Newport Amateur Operatic Society mount performances at the Lyceum Theatre, Newport
- ❖ **1905** Conductor FW Burpitt leaves for Canada and Newport Amateur Operatic Society did not continue
- ❖ **1920** Autumn: Chance meeting of Herbert Harte and Harold Williams creates interest in forming an operatic society
- ❖ **1920** December: Committee formed, advertisement in the local press, followed by a meeting in the Town Hall which agrees to form Newport Operatic Society
- ❖ **1921** December: The Society's first Performance - *Mikado*
- ❖ **1935** Newport Operatic Society decides to move to the 'more modern' type of musical. *Desert Song* produced in December
- ❖ **1936** The Society organises a broadcast of Edward VIII's Abdication Speech to interrupt a performance of *The Vagabond King*
- ❖ **1937-1938** The Society moves to the Empire Theatre - a venue with double the capacity of the Lyceum
- ❖ The War Years:
- ❖ **1942** the Empire Theatre burns down
- ❖ **1948** Performances resume with a production of *The Desert Song*. Producer Harry Winton taken ill and prompt girl Maisie Griffiths steps in
- ❖ **1949** Maisie Griffiths becomes the Society's regular producer with a 'triumphal' production of *Nina Rosa*
- ❖ **1958** Local rivals, The Standard Telephones and Cables Operatic Society, is established

- ❖ **1960** Newport Operatic Society performs its last show at the Lyceum theatre which was sold and later partially demolished
- ❖ **1961** The Society finds a temporary home at the Little Theatre, Dock Street. Technical problems at this converted chapel are overcome and Maisie Griffiths produces one of its best shows – *South Pacific* with Ian Frost and Margaret Shead
- ❖ **1962** Norman Abraham, Newport Operatic's first Mikado in 1921, gives up the post of General Honorary Secretary. He becomes the Society's first Honorary life Member
- ❖ **1963** December: Long standing Musical Director, Arthur Holland, dies a few days before the opening night of *The Belle of New York*. Billy Martin, who had played in the pit at the 1921 performance of *Mikado*, conducts the show
- ❖ **1964** Maisie Griffiths announces she wants to restrict out-of-London commitments and could no longer undertake the Society's productions - though she returns in the 1970s
- ❖ **1967** Newport Operatic moved to the new Dolman theatre. *Kismet* was the first production
- ❖ **1973** Dorothy Atwell Clarke becomes the first female Musical Director of Newport Operatic Society – *The Dancing Years* was her first show in the role
- ❖ **2004** Newport Operatic Society produces Ivor Novello's *The Dancing Years* – the last production of an old romantic show.

List of Shows Performed by Newport Operatic Society

1921	*The Mikado*
1922	*The Gondoliers*
1923	*Yeomen of the Guard*
1924	*Iolanthe*
1925	*Princess Ida*
1926	*Trial by Jury/*
	The Pirates of Penzance
1927	*Utopia Limited*
1928	*The Rebel Maid*
1929	*The Mikado*
1930	*Merrie England*
1931	*The Gondoliers*
1932	*Iolanthe*
1933	*Patience*
1934	*Yeomen of the Guard*
1935	*Desert Song*
1936	*The Vagabond King*
1937	*Rose Marie*
1938	*The New Moon*
1948	*Desert Song*
1949	*Nina Rosa*
1950	*Countess Maritza*
1951	*The Arcadians*
1952	*Rio Rita*
1953	*Showboat*
1954	*The Quaker Girl*
1955	*The New Moon*
1956	*The Dancing Years*

1957	*White Horse Inn*
1958	*Perchance to Dream*
1959	*The Merry Widow*
1960	*Rose Marie*
1961	*South Pacific*
1962	*The Dubarry*
1963	*The Belle of New York*
1964	*Annie Get Your Gun*
1965	*The Pajama Game*
1966	*The Vagabond King*
1967	*Kismet*
1968	*My Fair Lady*
1969	*The Arcadians*
1970	*Calamity Jane*
	Die Fledermaus
1971	*South Pacific*
1972	*Naughty Marietta*
1973	*The New Moon*
	The Bartered Bride
1974	*The Gypsy Baron*
1975	*Desert Song*
1976	*Me and My Girl*
	The Dancing Years
1977	*HMS Pinafore*
	The Merry Widow
1978	*Frederica*
	Iolanthe
1979	*The Mikado*
1980	*The Pirates of Penzance*
	Orpheus in the Underworld
1981	*Die Fledermaus*

	The Gondoliers
1982	*The Yeomen of the Guard*
	La Belle Helene
1983	*Free as Air*
	King's Rhapsody
1984	*Iolanthe*
	Brigadoon
1985	*Carousel*
	Waltzes from Vienna
1986	*Hello Dolly*
1987	*Oklahoma*
	The Merry Widow
1988	*Showboat*
	Viva Mexico
1989	*White Horse Inn*
	Pirates of El Penzance
1990	*Gigi*
	Orpheus in the Underworld
1991	*South Pacific*
	The Dancing Years
1992	*Die Fledermaus*
	Guys and Dolls
1993	*High Society*
	The Pajama Game
1994	*My Fair Lady*
	Oklahoma
1995	*Music Man*
	King's Rhapsody
1996	*Anything Goes*
1997	*Me and My Girl*
	Singing in the Rain

1998	Guys and Dolls
	Pickwick
1999	Gigi
	The Mikado
2000	The Merry Widow
	Oliver!
2001	Hello Dolly
	Calamity Jane
2002	Brigadoon
	Irene
2003	The Pajama Game
	Carousel
2004	The Dancing Years
	Scrooge
2005	Half a Sixpence
	Annie
2006	South Pacific
	Jekyll and Hyde
2007	The Wizard of Oz
	Oliver!
2008	Thoroughly Modern Millie
	Oklahoma
2009	There's No Business Like Show Business
	Anything Goes
2010	Revue – 90 Glorious Years
	Hot Mikado
2011	Jesus Christ Superstar
	The Sound of Music
2012	Jekyll and Hyde
	Calamity Jane
2013	Annie

	A Christmas Carol
2014	*Chess*
2015	*Oliver!*
	Sunset Boulevard
2016	*Old Tyme Music Hall*
2017	*Stage2Screen*
	The Most Wonderful Time of the Year
2018	*Little Shop of Horrors*
	Their Sacrifice for Our Future
2019	*The Greatest of Shows*